I Like to Dance

By Alex Kimathi
Illustrated by Evgeniia Smolentseva

Library For All Ltd.

We dance the *Dodo*.

We dance *Lingala*.

We dance *Kapuka*.

We dance *Azonto*.

We dance *Mugithi*.

We dance the *Isukuti*.

We dance *Genge*.

We dance *Taarab*.

We dance the *Mwomboko*.

We dance happily!

About the contributors

Library For All works with authors and illustrators from around the world to develop diverse, relevant, high-quality books. Visit libraryforall.org for the latest news on writers' workshop events, submission guidelines and other creative opportunities.

Did you enjoy this book?

We have hundreds more expertly curated original stories to choose from.

We work in partnership with authors, educators, cultural advisors, governments and NGOs to bring the joy of reading to people everywhere.

Did you know?

We create global impact in these fields by embracing the United Nations Sustainable Development Goals.

libraryforall.org

You're reading Level 1

Learner – Beginner readers

Start your reading journey with short words, big ideas and plenty of pictures.

Level 1 – Rising readers

Raise your reading level with more words, simple sentences and exciting images.

Level 2 – Eager readers

Enjoy your reading time with familiar words, but complex sentences.

Level 3 – Progressing readers

Develop your reading skills with creative stories and some challenging vocabulary.

Level 4 – Fluent readers

Step up your reading skills with playful narratives, new words and fun facts.

Level 5 – Curious readers

Discover your world through science and stories.

Level 6 – Adventurous readers

Explore your world through science and stories.

Library For All is an Australian not for profit organisation with a mission to make knowledge accessible to all via an innovative digital library solution. Visit us at libraryforall.org

I Like to Dance

First published 2024

Published by Library For All Ltd
Email: info@libraryforall.org
URL: libraryforall.org

This project was delivered with the support of Edmund Rice Foundation Australia.

Original illustrations by Evgeniia Smolentseva

I Like to Dance
Kimathi, Alex
ISBN: 978-1-923339-75-0
SKU04515

www.ingramcontent.com/pod-product-compliance
Lightning Source LLC
Chambersburg PA
CBHW042344040426
42448CB00019B/3401
9781923339750